PLAY SPIRITUALS

Best-loved tunes from the Deep South
Beliebte Stücke des Americanischen Süden
Les plus beaux airs des Etats du Sud

for trumpet/clarinet/tenor or alto saxophone with piano
für Trompete/Klarinette/Tenor- oder Altsaxophon und Klavier
pour trompette/clarinette/saxophon alto ou ténor et piano

arranged by Alan Gout

© 1994 by Faber Music Ltd
First published in 1994 by Faber Music Ltd
3 Queen Square, London WC1N 3AU
Cover design by Studio Gerrard
Music drawn by Christopher Hinkins
Printed in England by Halstan & Co Ltd
All rights reserved

ISBN 0 571 51457 X

Contents · Inhalt · Table

Swing Low Sweet Chariot 2
Little David Play 4
This Train 6
I Know the Lord's Laid His Hands on Me 8
By an' By 10
Joshua Fit' the Battle of Jericho 12
Go Tell it on the Mountains 14
Ev'ry Time I Feel the Spirit 16
Sometimes I Feel like a Motherless Child 18
Down by the Riverside 20

Swing Low Sweet Chariot

Little David Play

This Train

I Know the Lord's Laid His Hands on Me

* Small notes *ad lib.*

By an' By

*or ♪

Joshua Fit' the Battle of Jericho

Go Tell it on the Mountains

Ev'ry Time I Feel the Spirit

Sometimes I Feel like a Motherless Child

Down by the Riverside